# One Room School Games

# TABLE OF CONTENTS

This book may be ordered from:

Pictorial Histories Distribution
1416 Quarrier Street
Charleston, WV 25301
(304) 342-1848

$9.95 plus $2.00 shipping

# FOREWORD

As a small girl growing up on Oppossum Creek near the town of Ansted in Fayette County, I made frequent visits to my Uncle Stanley and Aunt Kathryn Hypes' home less than a mile away. There I would join my several cousins for many hours of pleasure. These visits are among my fondest memories.

On weekends or after all the chores had been completed for a day, we would gather in the backyard to play games. After dusk, my uncle would light the old kerosene lamp on the parlor mantle and it would be indoor play time. We would listen to stories and play games for hours at a time until my uncle reached for the family Bible to read a chapter to us, as he did every night. Then he would blow out the lamp flame, as we scattered in the direction of our beds.

It was this influence on my early life that has renewed my interest in the "one-room school games" of yesteryear. These games have nearly been forgotten by families of today. It was only after my Aunt Kathryn had raised her family that she returned to college and received her degree. She taught in the one-room Legg School on Stringtown Road for many years. The games that appear here are as she and others have told them to me. Perhaps some of our readers will help revive the old children's games that were played before the arrival of television and other forms of modern entertainment. Some can be played indoors, some outdoors, some in the snow, and others almost anywhere.

# JUMP ROPE RHYMES

(Usually played outside by three or more children but can also be played alone.) A long piece of rope is held by two children at opposite ends and swung around in a circular motion with the rope almost or barely touching the ground in the middle. A child stands at the middle of the rope and jumps over it as it swings beneath him. If the rope is long enough, two or more children sometimes jump at the same time. To jump alone, a shorter piece of rope is used. The child grasps each end of the rope, swings it in a circular motion over his head and under his feet and around and around, jumping over it each time it passes beneath him. While jumping rope, the children usually chant a rhyme. Some of these jingles include instructions to the jumper and those turning the rope. Many end when a jumper misses, meaning he trips over the rope or fails to jump over it.

# JUMP ROPE RHYMES

## CINDERELLA

Cinderella dressed in yellow,
Went down town to see her fellow;
How many kisses did he give her?
One, two, three . . . (Jumper continues to count until he misses).

## DOWN BY THE RIVER

Down by the river where the green grass grows
   sat (a girl's name) as pretty as a rose.
She sang, she sang so sweet and along came
   (a boy's name) and kissed her on the cheek.
How many kisses did she get?
One, two, three . . . (Jumper continues to count until he misses.)

## TEDDY BEAR

Teddy bear, teddy bear, turn around;
   (Jumper turns around.)
Teddy bear, teddy bear, touch the ground;
   (Jumper touches the ground.)
Teddy bear, teddy bear, read the news;
   (Jumper holds his hands as if reading a newspaper.)
Teddy bear, teddy bear, skid-da-do.
   (Jumper runs out from under the rope.)

## JOHNNY OVER THE OCEAN

Johnny over the ocean,
Johnny over the sea,
Johnny broke the sugar bowl,
And blamed it on me;
I told Ma;
Ma told Pa;
Pa gave Johnny H-O-T.
   (The rope is turned faster and faster until the jumper misses).

# JUMP ROPE RHYMES

### BLONDIE AND DAGWOOD

Blondie and Dagwood went downtown,
  Blondie bought an evening gown.
Cookie got a pair of shoes,
  and Alexander spread the news.

### GRACE, GRACE

Grace, Grace dressed in lace,
  Went upstairs to powder her face.
How many boxes did she use?
  1, 2, 3, etc. . . . (count until child misses)

### MABEL, MABEL

Mabel, Mabel, set the table,
  Don't forget the Red Hot Pepper!!
(Turn the rope as fast as you can)

### HOUSE FOR RENT

House for rent, inquire within,
  When I move out, Let _____ move in.
(Child names next child to jump)

### APPLE, APPLE

Apple, apple on the tree,
  Tell me who my beau shall be.
A, B, C, D, etc. . . . (Continue until child misses)

# JUMP ROPE RHYMES

## MR. LINCOLN

Mr. Lincoln, Mr. Lincoln
What on earth have you been drinking?
Smells like turkey, tastes like wine,
Oh my gosh, it's turpentine!

## MRS. BROWN

Mrs. Brown went downtown with her stockings down
She gave me a nickle,
To buy me a pickle
The pickle was sour
She gave me a flower
The flower was yellow
She gave me a fellow
The fellow was sick
She gave me a kick
The kick was hard
She gave me a card
and on that card said, "Red Hot Pepper!"
(the rope is turned very fast on Red Hot Pepper)

## CANDY SHOP

I met my boyfriend at the candy shop,
He bought me ice cream, he bought me cake
He took me home with a bellyache.
Mama, Mama, I feel sick,
Call the doctor quick, quick, quick!
Doctor, doctor will I die?
Count to five and you'll be alive
1-2-3-4-5, I'm alive!

# JUMP ROPE RHYMES

## JOHNNY OVER THE OCEAN

Johnny over the ocean, Johnny over the sea,
  Johnny broke a milk bottle and blamed it on me.
I told Ma, Ma told Pa,
  Johnny got a lickin', so Ha, Ha, Ha.
How many lickings did he get?
  (Count until child misses)

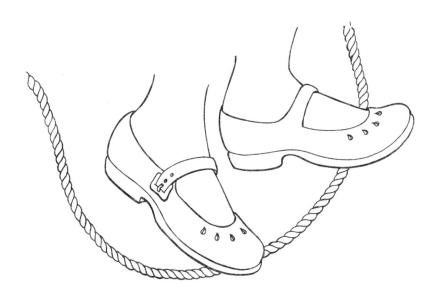

# JUMP ROPE RHYMES

## MAMA, MAMA, I FEEL SICK
Mama, Mama, I feel sick;
Send for the doctor,
Quick, Quick, Quick.
How many pills will he give me?
One, two, three . . . (Jumper continues to count until he misses.)

## WORMS IN THE JELLY BOWL
Worms in the jelly bowl, Wiggle, Waggle, Wiggle
  Worms in the jelly bowl, Wiggle, Waggle, Wiggle
I'm Mae West, I try to do my best
  Worms in the jelly bowl, Wiggle, Waggle, Wiggle.

## PEEL AN ORANGE
Peel an orange, round and round,
  See if you can touch the ground;
If you jump to twenty-two
  Another turn will be given to you!

## MY MOTHER, YOUR MOTHER
My mother, your mother, live across the street,
  Eighteen, Nineteen, Chestnut Street.
Every night they have a fight and this is what they say:
  Acka backa soda cracker, Acka backa boo.
In comes (next child's name) and out goes you! (runs out)

## CHARLIE CHAPLIN
Charlie Chaplin went to France
  To teach the ladies how to dance,
First the heel, then the toe,
  Around and around and around you go.
(Do these as jump: Salute to the Captain, Bow to the Queen,
  Touch the bottom of the submarine.)

## RING, RING — WHO HAS THE RING?

All form a circle. A string is tied to make a circle about the size of the circle made by the players standing almost shoulder to shoulder. A ring or washer is placed on the string. Each player keeps her hands moving as if she were passing the ring from one hand to another and then to the player next to her. This goes on constantly. The player in the center watches and hopes to "catch" the one who really has the ring. Usually 30 seconds or so is allowed before the player in the center must call out "Ring, Ring, Who has the Ring" and all stop the hand movement. The player in the center has three guesses to name the player. If he guesses correctly on one of his three guesses, that player becomes IT.

# SCRUB

Whenever someone had any kind of ball, a board would be found for a bat and a game of SCRUB or WORK UP ball would get underway.

At the beginning of recess or after lunch had been eaten, someone would yell, "first batter," then someone else would call, "second batter," "third batter," "catcher," "pitcher," "first base," "second base," "third base" and that was as far as the positions usually went.

When a batter made an out, that player had to take the last named position. The catcher became one of the batters, and the pitcher became the catcher, etc.


# PLUNDER

Sides were chosen.

A plank line was laid, and a team lined up on each side of the plank line.

Twenty-five or thirty feet from the line on each side was a pile of ten or a dozen sticks.

Players tried to get to the opposing team's stick pile without being tagged. If successful, that player took a stick and put it on that player's stick pile. If unsuccessful, that player (tagged) had to stay on the opposing team's stick pile until a player from his team reached him without being tagged.

When all the sticks were on one pile, that team was winner.


# SARDINES

4 to 20 players. One player hides and the others must hunt for him individually. As each player discovers hiding place, he joins the player hiding there. The hunt continues until all players have found and crowded into the hiding place. The last one to discover the hide-out becomes next hider.

# LONDON BRIDGE IS FALLING DOWN

Two players are the BRIDGE. They each silently pick a favorite color, fruit, or something else. These choices are known only to the two players who are the BRIDGE. They stand slightly apart, facing each other, clasping each other's hands head high to represent a bridge. The other players then crawl under the BRIDGE while everyone sings:

London Bridge is falling down,
Falling down, falling down;
London Bridge is falling down,
My fair lady.

When the final word, "lady," is sung, the BRIDGE drops to capture a player in their connected arms. The captured player is then told to choose between the two favorites previously picked by the two BRIDGE players. (Which favorite belongs to which BRIDGE player is not revealed until after the captured player whispers his guess.) The captured player then gets behind the BRIDGE player whose choice agreed with his, holding him around the waistline.

After all players are caught and lined up on one side or the other, holding the team member in front of them by the waist, there is a TUG OF WAR. The team which pulls the other team over to its side is the winner.

# BASE

One person is IT. IT is stationed at a base represented by a pail, rope, or other object. All other players are at the opposite end of the field. IT yells, "Run!" They all run toward the base, trying to reach it safely without being tagged by IT. All who are tagged join IT's side. This is repeated until only one is left untagged; then he becomes IT and the game begins anew.

# BAD MAN

The BAD MAN is stationed on one side of a field. All others are at the other end. They call back and forth.

Bad Man:     "What are you doing down there?"
Group:       "Stealing grapes."
Bad Man:     "What would you do if the bad man came along?"
Group:       "Knock him down and spit in his face."

The BAD MAN races to catch as many as he can, when they exchange places. All he catches then become a BAD MAN. Play continues until all except one are caught. The one remaining then becomes the BAD MAN and the game begins anew.

# RUN SHEEPY RUN

Players choose sides and one side decides where home will be. They draw a map in the dirt and then hide. The other side has to find them before they reach home free.

# POTATO RELAY

Divide players into teams. The first player is given a large tablespoon and a potato. He must carry the potato in the spoon to a goal line 10 to 15 feet distant and back, then hand the spoon with the potato in it to the second player who repeats the action. If a potato is dropped, the team must start over from the beginning. The first team to finish wins.

# HINDU TAG

In this safety tag game, any player is safe from "it" as long as he is on his knees with his forehead touching the ground.

# SANTA'S PACK

Players sit in circle and each player is given name of some toy in Santa's pack: sled, doll, soldier, ball, etc. One player is Santa. He marches in and around the circle, calling out names of toys, one at a time. As each name is called, that toy gets up and follows Santa. When Santa calls, "Santa's pack is full!" all players, including Santa, rush to get a seat. Sitting players who have not been called must find new seats, too. The player left without a seat becomes Santa.

# NUT RACE

Each player pushes a nut with a pencil in hand, or a toothpick held between the teeth, across the floor to a goal line and back. First player or team to finish wins.

# OPPOSITES

The players sit in a circle and "it" stands in the center. "It" points to a player, who must immediately do the opposite of whatever "it" is doing. If "it" pulls his right ear, the player must pull his own left ear. If "it" smiles, the player frowns. "It" might rub his head, scratch his left foot, wave his right hand, pretend to sit, etc. When a player makes a mistake, he becomes "it".

# NO BEARS OUT TONIGHT

This is a form of tag with one player being "it" and trying to tag the other players before they reach home tree. It is played at twilight and before they start running, the players sing out "No Bears Out Tonight."

# HOPSCOTCH

(Individual accomplishment. Usually played outdoors.) A diagram with eight numbered spaces is drawn with chalk on a sidewalk or driveway or with a stick in the dirt. Through the years, several variations on the diagram have been used. The players each find a flat object such as a piece of glass, pebble, or small stick to use as an individual marker. They then line up to take turns hopping up and back on the diagram.

Here is the hopping procedure, disregarding the presence of a marker: Spaces 1 and 2; 4 and 5; 7 and 8 — hop into both spaces simultanteously with one foot in each of the two spaces. Spaces 3 and 6 — hop into on one foot. Starting with spaces 1 and 2, the hopping procedure would go like this: two feet, one foot, two feet, one foot, two feet, turn around in the air, two feet, one foot, two feet, one foot, two feet, then out of the diagram.

In actual play, a marker would be in one of the spaces. The player would not hop in the space occupied by his marker on the trip up the diagram. On his return trip, he would pick up his marker from the space ahead, then hop into that space and continue on. For example, if the marker is in space 5, the player would hop from space three into space 4 on one foot, then into space 6 on one foot, skipping space 5. On the return, the player would stand on one foot in space 6 to pick up the marker in space 5, then hop simultaneously into spaces 4 and 5, with one foot in each space.

To begin the game, the first player in line tosses his marker into square number 1. If it lands outside the square or on a line, he misses his turn and goes to the end of the line. If the marker lands in space number 1, the player then hops on one foot into space number 2 and then into number 3. He then lands on both feet simultaneously, with his right foot in space number 5 and his left in space number 4. Next he hops on one foot into space number 6 and then lands on both feet simultaneously, with his right foot in space number 8 and his left foot in space 7. He hops back to space 2 on one foot, except in spaces 4 and 5. Standing on one foot in space 2, he bends over and picks up his marker from space 1, straightens up, hops into space 1, then hops outside the diagram. He then tosses his marker into space 2 and hops again. He progresses through each number until he misses. Then he goes to the end of the line to await his next turn leaving his marker where he left off. A player misses when he touches a line with his foot or hand or any other part of his body.

The game continues until a player has successfully thrown his marker in all eight spaces and successfully hopped up and back on the diagram, picking up his marker on each successive return trip. When hopping, players disregard markers other than their own. They cannot brace themselves with their other hand or knee when reaching to pick up their marker.

## ANDY OVER (or ANTE OVER)

A group of children stands on each side of the schoolhouse. One group throws a ball over the building as they yell, "Andy over!" Somebody on the opposite side tries to catch the ball and runs to the other side to join that team if he catches it. The side with the largest number at the end of the game wins. A softball is usually used in this game.

## ROCKY BRANCH "ANTE OVER"

An equal number was placed on each side of the school building and if a ball could be caught in the air or on the first bounce, that person and the rest of the team would run to the other side of the building and anyone hit with the ball became a member of their team. This was played with a sponge ball like the one used in "burn out".

# BURN OUT

Burn out was played with a sponge ball, a bat and two bases. One team consisted of two players against all others. There was only two bases, homeplate and another one 100 to 150 feet away. When the batter hit the ball, the fielder either caught the ball in the air or hit the runner with the ball. The second player would then come to bat, the first batter would have to return home when that batter hit. The fielder who hit the batter or caught the ball would then exchange places with the batter or runner who was put out.

# SQUAT TAG

The person who is IT can catch anyone not squatting. When someone is caught not squatting, he becomes IT. The winner is the one never tagged. Players usually only squat when IT gets near them. They run and stand to tease IT.

# ROCK TAG

Same game as squat tag, except that players cannot be caught when they are standing on a rock.

# TOSS THE BALL

The players stand in a circular formation. IT stands inside the circle and tosses a ball at the other players' feet. Those in the circle hold hands so that they cannot use their hands to keep the ball inside the circle. Only their feet are used to stop the ball. The two players who let the ball get outside the circle between them are eliminated from the game. This procedure continues until the last two are trying to keep the ball inside. They are the winners. A medium size rubber ball is used for this game.

## RED ROVER

One person is RED ROVER and stands at one end of a field. The others stand at the opposite end of the field. End and side boundaries are designated. Someone says: "Red Rover, Red Rover, we dare you to come over." RED ROVER then runs to the opposite end of the field and tags as many players as possible. To be "safe" the players must reach the opposite end of the field where RED ROVER started without going out of the side boundaries. Those caught or chased out of bounds join RED ROVER at his end of the field and help him catch others in the next round. This continues until all but one are caught. The remaining person wins and then becomes RED ROVER for the next game.

## RING-AROUND-A-ROSIE

Players form a circle with one player in the center. The circle walks, singing:

Ring-around-a-Rosie;
Pockets full of posies;
Blue bird, black bird,
SQUAT!

The last one seen to squat goes inside the circle until the game is repeated and the next loser takes his place there. Only one person stands inside the circle at a time.

## GOING TO NEW ORLEANS

All the players sit in a circle. One starts by saying, "I'm going to New Orleans and I'm going to take my guitar." Another says they are going to take their horse and another their hat, etc. Then the first says he is going to play his guitar. Everyone is then going to play their item. The second will then ride his horse and everyone is going to ride his item. The third will wear his hat and everyone is then going to wear their item.

## HOP, STEP AND JUMP

A line of players hop, then step and then jump to see who can go the farthest.

### LEAP FROG

Children line up one behind the other. They are on their hands and knees. Another child gets at the end of the line and jumps over all the others one at a time. If the jumper can jump over all without falling, the jumper then takes the front position on hand and knees and the last person in the line becomes the jumper. When a jumper falls, he is out of the game.

# THE FARMER IN THE DELL

The players form a circle. Someone is picked to be the farmer and stands in the center of the circle. Then, the circle walks and sings, reversing direction at the start of each verse:

The farmer in the dell;
The farmer in the dell;
Hi, Ho, the dairyo;
The farmer in the dell.

The farmer takes a wife;
The farmer takes a wife;
Hi, Ho, the dairyo;
The farmer takes a wife.

During the second verse of the song, the farmer takes the hand of someone in the circle, and that person joins him in the center and becomes the wife.

The verse is sung four more times, changing the first two lines in sequence:

The wife takes a child;
The child takes a nurse;
The nurse takes a dog;
The dog takes a bone.

During the singing of each subsequent verse, a new person is picked from the circle by the "child," "nurse," and "dog," in turn, to join the group in the center. Additional verses can be created, and the game can go on and on. If the game is to be repeated, eventually, the circle sings: "The bone (or last thing named) stands alone . . . " Everyone in the center except the last person chosen to enter it then rejoins the circle. The last person then becomes the farmer and the game begins anew.

# FOX AND GOOSE

(Usually played in the snow with five players.) A diagram is drawn in the snow (a circle and an inner circle). One child wears a sign on his back or chest reading, "FOX." The other four players are "GEESE." As the game begins, the FOX stands in the inner circle and the GEESE stand on the outer circle, positioned as the four main points on a compass: north, south, east, and west. The FOX attempts to catch a GOOSE. The GEESE are only safe from being caught when they are inside the inner circle. The FOX chases the GEESE until he catches one. The GOOSE caught then becomes the FOX and the game starts anew.

## WHO'S GOT THE THIMBLE?

The group sits in a circle. The student who is IT holds a thimble in his hand. Each of the others holds his hands together to receive the thimble, without revealing that he has or doesn't have the thimble, while the thimble is presumably passed from one person to the next around the entire circle. Any player, including the first one, may keep the thimble hidden in his hands and merely pretend to pass it on. The group watches closely, trying to detect whether or not the thimble is actually passed. After everyone has passed, or pretended to pass, the thimble, IT says, "Who's got the thimble?" Each player, in turn, guesses. The one guessing right is then IT for the next game. If no one guesses correctly, IT says, "Rise Thimble." The player holding the thimble reveals it and it is then IT for the next game.

# MOTHER MAY I?

A starting line and a finish line are designated. One person plays MOTHER. MOTHER stands or sits at the finish line. All others line up at the starting line. Players progress from the starting line to the finish line according to the game rules. MOTHER commands each player, in turn; for example: "Mary, take three elephant steps; John take one baby step; Susie, do one somersault; Bill, hop on one foot twice backwards," etc. Before obeying the command, the person must say, "Mother may I? If he fails to say this before doing as told, he must go back to the starting line. If he responds properly, MOTHER then gives a command to the next player. This process continues until someone forgets to say, "Mother may I?" The forgetful one must go back to the starting line. The winner is the first one to cross the finish line.

# THE MULBERRY BUSH

A circle is formed; and, holding hands, the children march around singing:

Here we go 'round the mulberry bush,
The mulberry bush, the mulberry bush;
Here we go 'round the mulberry bush,
So early in the morning.

Then the children stand still, unclasp hands, and pretend to be washing clothes on an old-fashioned scrub board (an up and down motion), while they sing:

This is the way we wash our clothes,
Wash our clothes, wash our clothes,
This is the way we wash our clothes,
So early in the morning.

# MUSICAL CHAIRS

(Usually played indoors.) A recording of a song (any song) must be played for this game, and a teacher or other non-player stops and starts the music at unspecified intervals. Chairs are placed in a circle, with one chair for each player except one. As long as the music plays, the players walk around the chairs. When the music stops, everyone scrambles for a chair. The one left without a chair is eliminated from the game. A chair is then removed, and the music starts again. This procedure continues until only one player, the winner, remains in the game.

# DROP THE HANDKERCHIEF

All the players stand or sit in a circle facing the center. One person is IT. IT steps out of his place and walks around the outside of the circle and drops the handkerchief behind someone. If that person does not see the handkerchief, he goes into the "mush pot" (inside circle). If he sees the handkerchief, he tries to catch IT before IT gets back to his place in the circle. If IT is caught, IT goes into the "mush pot," and the player who caught him becomes IT. If not caught, IT drops the handkerchief behind another person. The object is to see how many players you can get into the "mush pot" without going in yourself. Everyone who remains out of the "mush pot" is a winner.

# PRETTY GIRL STATION

The players divide into two groups, the same number on each team. The teams stand on opposite ends of a field and yell back and forth:

Side I:  Here we come.
Side II: Where're you from?
Side I:  Pretty Girl Station.
Side II: What's your trade?
Side I:  Lemonade.
Side II: Get to work and show us some.

Side I does the motion of doing something, such as reading, washing, ironing, sewing, or whatever. If Side II players guess the task correctly, they try to tag as many opposing players as possible while exchanging sides. Those tagged join the opposing team. Roles are reversed in the next round. The team with the most players at the end of the game wins.

# DUCK, DUCK, GOOSE

The players form a circle, either standing or sitting, facing toward the inside of the circle. Someone is picked to be IT. IT walks around outside the circle, touches someone on the back and says, "Duck." He repeats this several times, picking players at random. At any time he wishes, IT switches and says, "Goose." When the player who was touched hears, "Goose," he chases IT. IT runs to the open area in the center of the circle of players. If he makes it there safely before the player chasing him tags him, then he remains IT and the game is resumed, the same as before. If the chaser tags IT before IT gets inside the circle, the chaser then becomes IT and the game resumes.

# GO IN AND OUT THE WINDOW

Players form a circle, holding hands. One person is IT and starts weaving in and out beside each person in the circle, as everyone sings:

Go in and out the window;
Go in and out the window;
Go in and out the window;
For we have gained the day.

Kneel down and face your lover;
Kneel down and face your lover;
Kneel down and face your lover;
For we have gained the day.

As the second verse is sung, IT kneels down in front of someone in the circle. Everyone then sings:

One kiss before I leave you;
One kiss before I leave you;
One kiss before I leave you;
For we have gained the day.

As the third verse is sung, IT rises, kisses his chosen one on the cheek, and becomes part of the circle. The one kissed is then IT, and the game is repeated as many times as desired.

# HIDE AND SEEK

A student is selected to be IT. IT counts to 100 while the others select individual hiding places. Then IT yells, "Ready or not; you shall be caught." IT searches for the others and as they are found, they are eliminated from the game. The last one found or the one who can't be found wins and beomes IT for the next game.

*Painting of old German post card of children playing Hide and Seek.*

# RUTH AND JACOB

(Inside game.) RUTH is IT. The RUTH player is blindfolded and put in the circle made by other players' clasped hands.

Silently the circle players push one from the circle into the center with RUTH. That player is JACOB. Jacob calls "Ruth." Quickly and as quickly as possible, Jacob moves to somewhere else in the circle. Ruth seeks Jacob and may call "Jacob" at any time. Jacob answers "Ruth."

When Ruth tags Jacob, then Ruth must identify who Jacob is. If two guesses are wrong, Ruth is still IT. If Jacob is identified correctly, Jacob becomes Ruth and is blindfolded and the game goes on.

# I SPY

(Inside game.) IT hides an object in plain sight while other players hide their eyes.

Then the players look for the hidden object and say I SPY when the object is located, but they may take a step or two away and look somewhere else as they say I SPY. The first I SPY person gets to hide for the next game.

# HOT POTATO

The object in this game is to make all sorts of pounding patterns with our "potato fists" at a speed that the other children cannot keep up with. The last one to be confused by the leader wins and takes over as the leader with his own patterns. The players can also make up counting rhymes to go with their patterns which creates some very twisted tongues.

# DON'T LAUGH

All the children sit in a circle and the first one to grin is "out." This goes on until there is only one left who is the winner. While the children are "out" they try to make the others grin.

# THREE DEEP

The players stand in a circle two deep (one in front of the other) facing center. There is a tagger and a runner who run outside the circle. The runner stops in front of a couple which makes the third one become the runner. If the runner is caught before he stops in front of a couple then he becomes the tagger and the tagger becomes the runner.

# WINK OR WINKUM

You form a circle of chairs with one player seated in every chair but one. A player stands behind every chair including the vacant one. The player standing behind the vacant chair winks at a seated player to come and fill the vacant chair. Then he, in turn, winks at someone to fill his chair. The object is to keep all the chairs filled.

## JUMPING THE OLD GRAPE VINE

If you don't have a jump rope you can use a grape vine. It will bend into all kinds of figures, but you sometimes get whacked on the head as you jump.

## TREASURE HUNT

The players hide notes that will eventually lead to the "treasure." "Each note tells the players where to go next.

## OLD MR. RED COAT

Players sit in a row. The one at the beginning of the row says, "Old Mr. Red Coat sent me to you," to the player beside of him. Then that player says, "What for to do?" The leader says, "To hammer one hammer as I do." They would then make a motion such as pounding one fist on their knee and each player down the row follows. The leader then goes to two hammers, which is both fists and then three hammers, which is both fists and one foot and so on.

## POOR OLD DEAD MAN

This game has to be played in the fall. One player lays on the ground and the other players cover him with leaves. They join hands and march around him chanting, "Poor old dead man, Poor old dead man." After so long the "dead man" rises up and catches someone. Then they have to be the "dead man."

## CORK THROW

Place a basket on a chair. Divide the players into teams. Each player stands 3 to 6 feet distant, throws 2 corks into the basket. The team with high score wins.

## DOGGIE AND HIS BONE

One player is the doggie and stands with his back to the rest of the players. You put an object that is the bone behind the doggie's back. One player goes up and "steals" the "bone." That player then hides the "bone." The "doggie" turns and faces the players and tries to guess who stole the "bone." If the "doggie" guesses the right person then that player has to go up and be the "doggie." If the "doggie" guesses wrong then he has to continue being the "doggie."

## I SEND MY SHIP A SAILING

A small pillow is thrown to a child and the sender says, "I send my ship a sailing and it's loaded with (a product starting with the sender's last initial). The receiver then throws the pillow to someone else and says the same thing, but if the "ship" is loaded with something other than a product starting with his last initial he has to sit in the middle. If he catches on he can catch the pillow and get out, but if he catches the pillow and still doesn't catch on to the "initial" he has to stay in the middle.

# OLD DUSTY MILLER

After choosing partners, the couples walk in a circle and sing the following song.

Oh, there was an old miller
Who lived by the mill
He worked all day
With a right good will
One hand on the hopper
The other on the sack,
The ladies step forward
And the gents step back.

At this point two circles are formed, one within the other. The girls walk in one direction and the boys walk in the opposite direction singing the following song.

Here we go a-sowing oats
Here we go a-sowing oats
Here we go a-sowing oats
And who will be the binder.

I have lost my true love
I have lost my true love
I have lost my true love
And here is where I find her.

New couples form by each boy pairing with the girl who is beside him when the song ends. Then the game begins again with the Old Miller song.


# BLIND MAN'S BLUFF

Someone is IT. IT is blindfolded and stands in the center of a circle formed by the other players. One from the circle walks close to IT. IT is allowed to touch the person and tries to guess who he is. If IT guesses right, the person who walked into the circle is IT for the next round. If he guesses incorrectly, IT tries again.

# HOT POTATO

Players form a circle and a potato is passed rapidly around the circle to the right. When the music stops, or the leader blows a whistle, the player holding the potato is out of the game. No player may hesitate in receiving the "hot" potato. For large groups, keep several potatoes passing. All players holding them when the stop signal comes are eliminated from the game. Remove one potato each time.

## RED LIGHT

At home base, IT closes eyes and begins to count. Other players run to hide. At any time IT can say "Red Light!" IT also whirls around with open eyes to see if all players have stopped. Any in motion have to return to home base and start out again.

When all are hidden, IT goes looking.

IT calls out name of discovered player, both race to home base; If IT wins, IT says "One, two, three on (names player)."

If player wins, that player calls out, "Free."

Whichever is decided on — first or last found is IT for next game.


## GUARD THE GATE

Players sit on the floor, arm's length apart. Each player guards the space to his right. The leader rolls a ball (a volleyball is good) toward the players. The object is not to let the ball go through the space you are guarding. Anyone letting it go through is out of the game.


## BLACK MAGIC

(For adults or children. Inside game.) Two players are wise to the game; one leaves the room and the other stays. The group in the room selects an object. The person who is out of the room does not know what it is but will be able to identify the object selected because the other person who is wise to the game and remained in the room will give him a secret cue, which only the two of them know. The other players are unaware that these two are working together.

# TIN CAN TOSS

You will need three 3 pound coffee cans that have been emptied and had one end removed. Place the cans single file on a flat surface. Mark a throwing line that is approximately four feet and directly across from the cans. Next, find a small rock for each player to toss. Players take turns from behind the throwing line and try to toss their rock into first bucket #1, then #2 and then #3. The first player to toss his or her rocks into all the buckets wins.

# HOME MADE SOAP BUBBLES

Mix a strong solution of dish detergent and water. Bend twist ties or pieces of wire into a wand shape and dip in the solution. Blow!

# SNOW ANGELS

Lay down in the snow. Move your arms up and down and your legs in and out. When you get up you will have an angel in the snow.

# RACING WHEELS

Find an old wheel rim and a stick for each child. Make a starting line and a finishing line. The children race from start to finish pushing the wheel rim with the stick. The first one to the finishing line wins.

# PIN TAIL ON DONKEY

Hang a picture of a donkey with no tail on wall. Blindfold a child and have him pin a tail on the donkey.

# DROP THE CLOTHESPIN IN THE BOTTLE

One child stands with a milkbottle between her feet and holds a handful of wooden clothespins. Holding the pins at waist level she tries to drop them one by one into the bottle. There are all sorts of variations, such as backwards, waist-high, chest-high, etc. The winner is the one who gets the most pins in the bottle. It is a great test of hand-eye coordination.

# STONE SCHOOL

A leader is appointed. The game is played on the front porch steps (ideally 4 or more steps - inside stairs may also be used).

Each player guesses which hand holds the stone, pebble or marble. If they guess correctly, they advance one step up. If they guess incorrectly, they remain at the bottom step or descend one step down.

The player who makes it all the way up - must now make it all the way down. If at the top - and guess incorrectly, they remain on that or on whatever step they are on, until guessing correctly. The player who makes it up and down all the steps - becomes the new leader.

# TIN CAN

IT hides eyes. Someone kicks the tin can and all players run to hide.

IT must go get the can and bring it back to home base. Then search for the hiders.

IT must keep a close watch on home base, for players can sneak in, kick the can and go hide again. IT must retrieve the can and begin the search again.

When IT finds a player, both race to home base. IT must say "One, two, three on _____" before the found player can kick the can.

When IT gets all the players tagged, first tagged player is it.


# OUTSIDE FRUIT BASKET

All players except one stand around two deep.

IT gives each player the name of a fruit (animal, vegetable, etc.)

IT then calls out the names of two fruits (or whatever).

Those players try to exchange places and IT also tries to get one of the places.

Next IT is the player who does not get one of the spots.

IT may also call out "front" or "back"; then all "front" players or all the "back" players change places and IT competes for one of the spots.


# SNOW FORTS AND WAR

Sides are formed.

Snow forts are built about twenty feet apart.

Snow balls are the ammunition.

Whenever a player shows self, the opposite side tries to hit that one with a snow ball. If hit, that one must change sides. When all players are on the same side, that side has won.

# ONE ROOM SCHOOL

In my memory I go walkin'
Down an old country lane,
Sometimes through the sunshine,
The snow and through the rain,
I stop when I come
To the little one room country school,
Where I learned readin, writin, and arithmetic,
And was taught the Golden Rule.

With the other children I go inside,
And before we take our seats,
The teacher has us bow our heads,
And the Lord's prayer we all repeat.
Then she reads from the Bible,
And we sing a song or two,
And pledge our allegiance to the Flag,
The old red, white and blue.

The school room always looks the same,
It never changed one bit,
And I can still recall,
The familiar things around in it.
The big round globe that took us,
To so many far away places,
The blackboard where we had,
Arithmetic and sometimes spelling races.

Webster's dictionary opened,
On a stand that was so tall,
George Washington's picture,
Hanging up front high on the wall.
The gray stone water cooler,
A big map that unrolled.
In the center of the room,
A pot bellied coal heating stove.

Pencil sharpener near a window,
Teachers old fashioned desk and chair,
Initials carved in the seats,
Around most every where.
Recitation bench where each class,
Had their lessons every day,
A little bell the teacher rang,
To call us children in from play.

A shelf that held an oil lamp,
And some extra reading books,
All the coats, caps and scarves,
Hanging on rusty metal hooks.
In my heart I'll always cherish
Those happy days of long ago,
And the little one room country school,
Where as a child I used to go.

— *Bernice L. Dunn*

**FOLLOWING PAGES:**

**Scene of Campbell School, A One Room
School in Barbour County, West Virginia.**

**Photo by Gerald Ratliff**

# STATUES

A leader takes the hand of one of the players and whirls them around and then suddenly releases their grip. The released player must freeze in exactly the position in which they find themselves at the end of the spin. The leader continues until all the players in the group are spun. The player who is left with the most ridiculous position, then becomes the new leader.

# SIMON SAYS

(Usually played indoors.) The children pick one of them to be SIMON. It is explained that everyone must obey a command given by SIMON, if he begins the command by saying the words, "Simon says." If he omits these words, the command is not to be obeyed. SIMON begins by saying: "Simon says stand up." The group obeys by standing. He then says, "Simon says sit down." The group obeys by sitting. He says, "Stand up." If anyone stands, he is eliminated from the game, because the words, "Simon says," were not said before the command. SIMON can give any number of other commands such as: smile, frown, clap your hands, don't move, run, turn around, and bend over. Unless the words, "Simon says," are said first, the command should not be obeyed, and those who obey it are "out." The game continues until all except one, the winner, are eliminated.

# DILLER DOLLAR

(Indoor game.) The verse goes:

Diller Dollar, Diller Dollar
As it passes from one hand into the other.
Is it here, is it there?
Is it fair to keep poor _____ (it) standing there?

This game is played with everyone sitting in a circle close together, with their left hand palm up and almost closed. A coin is passed from one person's palm to the one on their right as the song is sung with "it" tyring to locate the coin. When "it" locates the coin, the person caught with the coin becomes "it" and the game continues.

## CROSSED OR UNCROSSED

The players sit in a circle and the leader takes a pair of scissors and passes them on to the next player saying, "I received these crossed and give them to you uncrossed." This player tries to figure out the catch, which has nothing to do with the scissors. The catch is that his arms or legs, etc. are crossed or uncrossed. The player that figures out the catch wins.

## BOBETY - BOB - BOB

The players sit in a circle and are numbered one to fifteen. The leader stands in the center and points to a player saying, "Bobety - Bob - Bob" and then counts to ten quickly. If the player does not say his number before the leader finishes then he becomes the leader. This game moves fast.

## GRANDMA BROWN DIED

This is a circle game. The leader begins by saying, "Grandma Brown died last night." They say this very sad and with much expression. The next player asks (very concerned), "How did she die?" The leader answers, "Going this way," as he pats his right knee with right hand. The players repeat the motion going around the circle. Then, next time around, same statement is said, patting both knees, then right, then left foot (with hands still going), then the head, etc. . . .

## BUTTON, BUTTON, WHO HAS THE BUTTON?

The players form a circle with one player in the middle. He/she has a button and the other players hold their hands in a praying hands position, pointed outward from the chest (rather than in the praying position). As the player in the center passes around the inside of the circle each player opens his/her hands slightly to receive the button should they be the lucky one that the center player chooses to pass the button to. After passing the button the center player than asks, "Button, button, who has the button? the player guessing the correct person then gets to distribute the button.

# QUAKER MEETING

Everyone sits in a circle and one child starts it off by whispering a sentence (preferable oddball) in his neighbor's ear so no one else can hear. Each listener passes on what he thinks he hears. If nothing is heard, then he has to make something up. The end of the circle announces what he heard and the first one then gives the original sentence. Then the second person in the circle starts a new sentence and so on.

## C. C. DOUBLE C.

The leader says, "See, see double see, I see something you don't see and it starts with (letter of the alphabet). The first one to guess it gets to name something for the others to guess.

## HOT AND COLD

One child hides an object such as a small ball. Others hunt for the object. If someone gets close to where it is hidden, the child who hid it, cries HOT, if someone gets far away, cries COLD. When object is discovered, the child discovering it gets to hide it and the game starts all over again.

## I'M GOING TO PACK MY TRUNK

Everyone is seated around the room. The person chosen to be IT, begins the game by saying: "I'm going to pack my trunk." Turns are taken around the room with everyone guessing what is in the trunk. IT must tell them what letter the answer begins with. When someone gets the correct answer, that person becomes IT and the game begins again.

## BUSHEL OF WHEAT, BUSHEL OF RYE

"IT" hides eyes. Everyone else hides. IT cries "bushel of wheat, bushel of rye, all not hid holler 'I'. Bushel of wheat, bushel of clover, all not hid can't hide over." IT opens eyes and finds all he can. The first one found, becomes IT and the game begins again.

## CENTER DODGE

Players sit in a circle with one player in the center. The players take turns rolling the ball and trying to hit the center player's feet. If he does hit them then they switch places and the one who hit the feet has to sit in the middle.

# TUG OF WAR

A line is drawn on the ground. Players are divided into two equal teams. A long rope or grapevine is grasped on opposite ends by the opposing teams, the players lined up behind each other. The center of the rope is over the center line on the ground. A signal is given to begin, and each team begins to pull against the other. The team that succeeds in pulling its opponents over the center line is the winner.

## BUZZ

All the players sit in a circle. The first player counts off 1, 2, 3, 4, etc. The player having 7 or a multiple of 7 (14, 21, 28, etc.) must say the word "Buzz" instead of the number. Any player saying 7 or a multiple of 7 is eliminated from the game. The last player in the game is the winner.

## THE ABC GAME

A player is chosen by drawing straws. He calls out a letter of the alphabet. Each of the other players in turn must name within 10 to 15 seconds a word that begins with that letter. Any player not doing so is out of the game. Once each player has taken a turn, the next one names any other letter of the alphabet and so on. No player may use a previously used word. The last remaining player is the winner. The game can use cities, countries, animals for variation.

## TIN CAN TELEPHONE

You need two good tin cans and a piece of string. Punch a hole in the bottom of both cans and connect the cans with the string. Tie a knot in each end of the string so the cans won't slip off. Give one can to a friend and "talk" to each other.

## HORSESHOE THROWING

You will need three-four good horseshoes and a stick. Pound the stick securely into the ground. Take turns tossing the horseshoes at the stick trying to ring the horseshoe around the stick.

# STONE, SCISSORS AND PAPER

There are three positions of the hand and fingers in which the player uses. A closed fist is a stone, two extended fingers are a pair of scissors, and an open palm is a piece of paper. Each player pounds his fist simultaneously with all the others, counting out loud up to the number three in unison. On the count of three each player makes one of the three gestures; stone, scissors, or paper.

In a game of two players, when both make the same gesture, it is a draw. If the gestures differ, they score in the following manner. Scissors win over paper because it can cut it. Paper wins over stone because it can wrap it. Stone wins over scissors because it can sharpen it.

The winner gets to slap the other players with his two fingers on their wrists. For a more genteel game, scores can be kept.

# HANGMAN

Two players. One player makes up a sentence and the other player may guess letters of the alphabet which he thinks is in the sentence. If player misses a correct letter, he gets one segment of the hanging drawn. When he misses enough letters to spell out "HUNG" the game is ended and the roles of players are reversed.

/I/-m/-----/--/---r------/--m-rr--/

ZBDFJK

I /_M/__ı__/_o/C___L___o_/_oMo__o_

The sentence was "I/am/going/to/Charleston/tomorrow."

# DOT & DASH

Usually two players, however three or four can play, make 16 to 25 dots on a paper or blackboard. Using different color inks or chalks, a player draws a line connecting any two dots. The next player does the same. The object is to connect enough dots to make a square. The one completing a square puts his initial in that square. The one having the most squares wins.

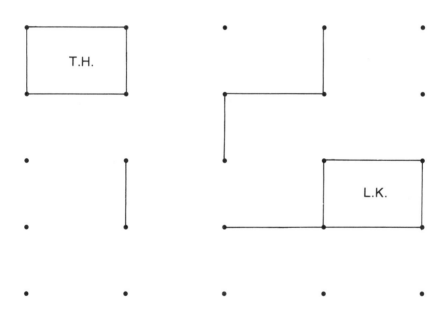

# MARBLES

Marbles were either played around a ring for "keeps" or for fun. When "keeps" was played, each player placed a certain number of marbles in the middle, then each player took turns trying to shoot marbles out of the ring. Any that were knocked out of the ring the shooter got to keep. Each person had a prized "shooter" and he could continue to shoot marbles out of the ring as long as a marble crossed the line after each shot.

A straight line is drawn on the ground. Players stand about seven to eight feet away and throw one marble trying to come the closest to the line. The one coming the closest keeps the other marbles on the ground.

A circle one foot in diameter is drawn on the ground. Each player places two marbles in the center of the circle. A player then drops his heaviest marble vertically trying to knock marbles outside the ring. He keeps all marbles knocked out. However, if no marbles are knocked out, the player leaves his shooter in the ring. The marbles are replaced in the center for the next player.

A line is marked and a sturdy cup is placed one arm's length away from the line. Each player beings the game with 5 marbles. Player one stands on the line and attempts to vertically drop each one of his marbles into the cup. The participant retrieves all of his marbles that landed outside the cup. This process is repeated until each player has had a turn. The player with the least number of remaining marbles (the participant who successfully dropped the most marbles into the cup) is allowed to keep the marbles that have collected in the cup.

Players may also be blindfolded while dropping their marbles.

A series of arches are cut out of a piece of cardboard, large enough for a marble to pass through. Each arch is given a number. Players shoot from a marked line, a designated number of marbles. The marbles passing through the arches are added up with the player having the highest score being the winner.

# INDEX

## JUMP ROPE RHYMES

## GAMES

# INDEX

## GAMES

# INDEX

## GAMES

## POEM

# NOTES

(Your favorite childhood games)

# NOTES

(Your favorite childhood games)